KU-538-724

the sun
and her flowers

also by rupi kaur
milk and honey

the sun
and her flowers

rupi kaur

SIMON &
SCHUSTER

London · New York · Sydney · Toronto · New Delhi

First published in the United States by Andrews McMeel Publishing,
a division of Andrews McMeel Universal, 2017
First published in Great Britain by Simon & Schuster UK Ltd, 2017
This edition published by Simon & Schuster UK Ltd, 2018

Copyright © Rupi Kaur, 2017

Illustrations and design by Rupi Kaur

The right of Rupi Kaur to be identified as the author of this work has been asserted
in accordance with the Copyright, Designs and Patents Act, 1988.

3 5 7 9 10 8 6 4

Simon & Schuster UK Ltd
1st Floor
222 Gray's Inn Road
London WC1X 8HB

www.simonandschuster.co.uk
www.simonandschuster.com.au
www.simonandschuster.co.in

Simon & Schuster Australia,
Sydney

Simon & Schuster India,
New Delhi

The author and publishers have made all reasonable efforts to contact copyright-holders
for permission, and apologise for any omissions or errors in the form of credits given.
Corrections may be made to future printings.

A CIP catalogue record for this book is available from the British Library

Hardback ISBN: 978-1-4711-7791-0
eBook ISBN: 978-1-4711-6583-2

Printed in China

Simon & Schuster UK Ltd are committed to sourcing paper that is made from
wood grown in sustainable forests and support the Forest Stewardship Council®,
the leading international forest certification organisation. Our books
displaying the FSC® logo are printed on FSC® certified paper.

to my makers
kamaljit kaur and suchet singh
i am. because of you.
i hope you look at us
and think
your sacrifices were worth it

to my stunning sisters and brother
prabhdeep kaur
kirandeep kaur
saaheb singh
we are in this together

you define love.

contents

bees came for honey
flowers giggled as they
undressed themselves
for the taking
the sun smiled

- *the second birth*

wilting

on the last day of love
my heart cracked inside my body

i spent the entire night
casting spells to bring you back

i reached for the last bouquet of flowers
you gave me
now wilting in their vase
one
by
one
i popped their heads off
and ate them

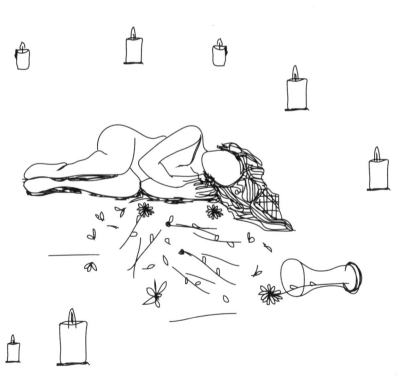

i stuffed a towel at the foot of every door
leave i told the air
i have no use for you
drew every curtain in the house
go i told the light
no one is coming in
and no one is going out

- *cemetery*

you left
and i wanted you still
yet i deserved someone
who was willing to stay

i spend days in bed debilitated by loss
i attempt to cry you back
but the water is done
and still you've not returned
i pinch my belly till it bleeds
have lost count of the days
sun becomes moon
and moon becomes sun
and i become ghost
a dozen different thoughts
tear through me each second
you must be on your way
perhaps it's best if you're not
i'm okay
no
i'm angry
yes
i hate you
maybe
i can't move on
i will
i forgive you
i want to rip my hair out
over and over and over again
till my mind exhausts itself into a silence

yesterday
the rain tried to imitate my hands
by running down your body
i ripped the sky apart for allowing it

- *jealousy*

in order to fall asleep
i have to imagine your body
crooked behind mine
spoon ladled into spoon
till i can hear your breath
i have to recite your name
till you answer and
we have a conversation
only then
can my mind
drift off to sleep

- *pretend*

it isn't what we left behind
that breaks me
it's what we could've built
had we stayed

i can still see our construction hats
lying exactly where we left them
pylons unsure of what to guard
bulldozers gazing out for our return
the planks of wood stiff in their boxes
yearning to be nailed up
but neither of us goes back
to tell them it is over
in time
the bricks will grow tired of waiting and crumble
the cranes will droop their necks in sorrow
the shovels will rust
do you think flowers will grow here
when you and i are off
building something new
with someone else

- the construction site of our future

i live for that first second in the morning
when i'm still half-conscious
i hear the hummingbirds outside
flirting with the flowers
i hear the flowers giggling
the bees growing jealous
when i turn over to wake you
the breaking starts
all over again
the panting
the wailing
the shock
of realising
you've left

- *the first week without you*

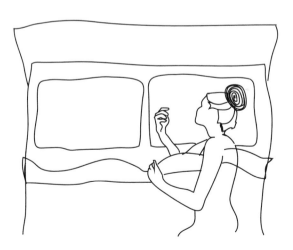

the hummingbirds tell me
you've changed your hair
i tell them i don't care
while listening to them
describe every detail

- *hunger*

i envy the winds
who still witness you

i could be anything
in the world
but i wanted to be his

i tried to leave many times
but as soon as i got away
my lungs buckled under the pressure
panting for air i'd return
perhaps this is why i let you
skin me to the bone
something
was better than nothing
having you touch me even if it was not kind
was better than not having your hands at all
i could take the abuse
i could not take the absence and
i knew i was beating a dead thing
but did it matter if
the thing was dead
if at the very least
i had it

- *addiction*

you break women in like shoes

loving you was breathing
but that breath disappearing
before it filled my lungs

- *when it goes too soon*

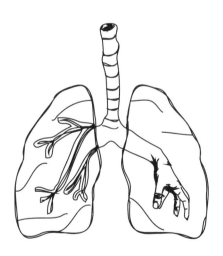

what love looks like

what does love look like the therapist asks
one week after the breakup
and i'm not sure how to answer her question
except for the fact that
i thought love looked so much like you

and that's when it hit me
that's when i realised how naive i had been
to place an idea so beautiful on the image of a person
as if anybody on this entire earth
could encompass all love represented
as if this emotion that seven billion people tremble for
would look like a five-foot-eleven
medium-sized brown-skinned guy
who likes eating frozen pizza for breakfast

so what does love look like the therapist asks again
this time interrupting my thoughts midsentence
and at this point i'm about to get up
and walk right out the door
except i paid far too much money for this hour
so instead i take a piercing look at her
the way you look at someone
when you're about to hand it to them
lips pursed tightly preparing to launch into conversation
eyes digging deeply into theirs
searching for all the weak spots

you most definitely know they have hidden somewhere
hair being tucked behind the ears
as if you have to physically prepare for a conversation
on the philosophies or rather disappointments
of what love looks like

well i tell her
i don't think love is him anymore
if love was him
he'd be here wouldn't he
if he was the one for me
wouldn't he be the one sitting across from me
i don't think love is him anymore i repeat
i think i just wanted something
that was bigger than myself
and when someone showed up
who could probably fit the part
i made it very much my intention
to make him my counterpart
and i lost myself to him
he took and he took
wrapped me in the word *special*
until i was convinced he had eyes only to see me
hands only to feel me
a body only to be with me
oh how he emptied me

well how does that make you feel
interrupts the therapist
well i said
it kinda makes me feel like shit

maybe we're all looking at it wrong
maybe we think it's something to search for out there
something that's supposed to crash into us
on our way out of an elevator
or slip into our chair at a cafe somewhere
appear at the end of an aisle at the bookstore
looking the right amount of sexy and intellectual
but i think love starts *here*
everything else is just desire and projection
of all our wants needs and fantasies
but those externalities could never work out
if we didn't turn inward and figure out
how to love ourselves in order to love other people

love does not look like a person
love is our actions
love is giving all we can
even if it's just the bigger slice of cake
love is understanding
we have the power to hurt one another
but we're going to do everything in our power
to make sure we don't
love is figuring out all the kind sweetness we deserve
and when someone shows up
saying they'll provide it as you do
but their actions seem to break you rather than build you
love is knowing who to choose

you cannot
walk in and out of me
like a revolving door
i have too many miracles
happening inside me
to be your convenient option

- *not your hobby*

you took the sun with you
when you left

i remained committed
long after you were gone
i could not lift my eyes
to meet eyes with someone else
looking felt like betrayal
what excuse would i have
when you came back
and asked where my hands had been

- *loyal*

when you plunged the knife into me
you also began bleeding
my wound became your wound
didn't you know
love is a double-edged knife
you will suffer the way you make me suffer

i think my body knew you would not stay

i long
for you
but you long
for someone else
i deny the one who wants me
cause i want someone else

- *the human condition*

i wonder
if i'm beautiful enough for you
or if i am beautiful at all
i change what i'm wearing
five times before i see you
wondering which pair of jeans will
make my body more tempting to undress
tell me
is there anything i can do
that'll make you think – *her*
she is so striking
she makes my body forget it has knees
write it in a letter and address it to
all the insecure parts of me
your voice alone drives me to tears
yours – telling me i am beautiful
yours – telling me i am enough

you're everywhere
except right here
and it hurts

show me a picture
i want to see the face of the woman
who made you forget the one you had at home
what day was it and
what excuse did you feed me
i used to thank the universe
for bringing you to me
did you enter her right as
i asked the almighty
to grant you all you wanted
did you find it in her
did you come crawling out of her
with what you couldn't in me

what draws you to her
tell me what you like
so i can practice

your absence is a missing limb

questions

there is a list of questions
i want to ask but never will
there is a list of questions
i go through in my head
every time i'm alone
and my mind can't stop itself from searching for you
there is a list of questions i want to ask
so if you're listening somewhere
here i am asking them

what do you think happens
to the love that's left behind
when two lovers leave
how blue do you think it gets
before it passes away
does it pass away
or does it still exist somewhere
waiting for us to come back
when we lied to ourselves
called this unconditional and left
which one of us hurt more
i shattered into a million little pieces
and those pieces shattered into a million more
crumbled into dust till
there was nothing left of me but the silence

tell me love
how did the grieving feel for you
how did the mourning hurt

how did you peel your eyes open after every blink
knowing i'd never be there staring back

it must be hard to live with *what-ifs*
there must always be this constant dull aching
in the pit of your stomach
trust me
i feel it too
how in the world did we get here
how did we live through it
and how are we still living

how many months did it take
before you stopped thinking of me
are you still thinking of me
if you are then
maybe i am too
thinking of you
thinking of me
with me
in me
around me
everywhere
you and me and us

do you still touch yourself to thoughts of me
do you still imagine my tiny naked body
pressed into yours
do you still imagine the curve of my spine
and how you wanted to rip it out of me
cause the way it dipped into
my perfectly rounded bottom
drove you crazy

baby
sugar baby
sweet baby
ever since we left
how many times did you pretend
it was my hand stroking you
how many times did you search for me in your fantasies
and end up crying instead of coming
don't you lie to me
i can tell when you're lying
cause there's always that little bit of
arrogance in your response

are you angry with me
are you okay
would you tell me if you're not
and if we ever see each other again
do you think you'd reach out and hold me
like you said you would
the last time we spoke and
you talked of the next time we would
or do you think we'd just look
shake in our skin as we pine to absorb
as much as we can of each other
cause by this time we've probably got
someone else waiting at home
we were good together weren't we
and is it wrong that
i'm asking you these questions
tell me love
that you have been looking
for these answers too

you call to tell me you miss me
i turn to face the front door of the house
waiting for a knock
days later you call to say you need me
but still aren't here
by this time
the dandelions on the lawn
are rolling their eyes in disappointment
the grass has declared you yesterday's news
what do i care if you love me
or miss me or need me
when you aren't doing anything about it
if i'm not going to be the love of your life
i'll be your greatest loss instead

where do we go from here my love
when it's over and i'm standing between us
whose side do i run to
when every nerve in my body is pulsing for you
when my mouth waters at the thought
when you are pulling me in just by standing there
how do i turn around and choose myself

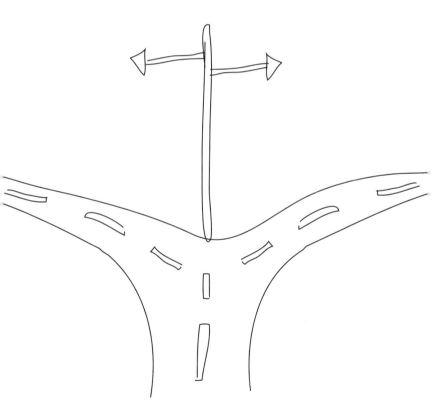

day by day i realise
everything i miss about you
was never there in the first place

- *the person i fell in love with was a mirage*

they leave
and act like it never happened
they come back
and act like they never left

- *ghosts*

i tried to find it
but there was no answer
at the end of the last conversation

- *closure*

you ask
if we can still be friends
i explain how a honeybee
does not dream of kissing
the mouth of a flower
and then settle for its leaves

- i don't need more friends

why is it
that when the story ends
we begin to feel all of it

rise
said the moon
and the new day came
the show must go on said the sun
life does not stop for anybody
it drags you by the legs
whether you want to move forward or not
that is the gift
life will force you to forget how you long for them
your skin will shed till there isn't
a single part of you left they've touched
your eyes
finally just your eyes
not the eyes which held them
you will make it to the end
of what is only the beginning
go on
open the door to the rest of it

- time

falling

i notice everything i do not have
and decide it is beautiful

i hardened under the last loss. it took something
human out of me. i used to be so deeply emotional i'd
crumble on demand. but now the water has made its
exit. of course i care about the ones around me. i'm just
struggling to show it. a wall is getting in the way. i used
to dream of being so strong nothing could shake me.
now. i am. so strong. that nothing shakes me.
and all i dream is to soften.

- *numbness*

yesterday
when i woke up
the sun fell to the ground and rolled away
flowers beheaded themselves
all that's left alive here is me
and i barely feel like living

- *depression is a shadow living inside me*

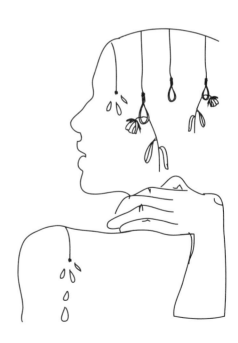

why are you so unkind to me
my body cries

cause you don't look like them
i tell her

you are waiting for someone
who is not coming back
meaning
you are living your life
hoping that someone will realise
they can't live theirs without you

- realisations don't work like that

a lot of times
we are angry at other people
for not doing what
we should have done for ourselves

- *responsibility*

why did you leave a door hanging open between my legs
were you lazy
did you forget
or did you purposely leave me unfinished

- *conversations with god*

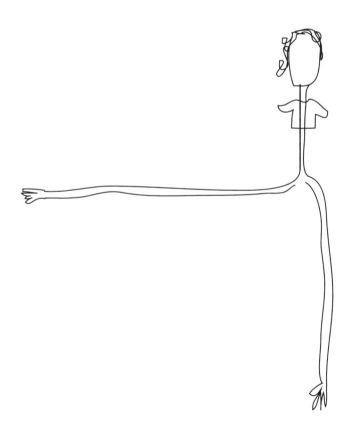

they did not tell me it would hurt like this
no one warned me
about the heartbreak we experience with friends
where are the albums i thought
there were no songs sung for it
i could not find the ballads
or read the books dedicated to writing the grief
we fall into when friends leave
it is the type of heartache that
doesn't hit you like a tsunami
it's a slow cancer
the kind that does not show up for months
has no visible signs
is an ache here
a headache there
but manageable
cancer or tsunami
it all ends the same
friend or lover
a loss is a loss is a loss

i hear a thousand kind words about me
and it makes no difference
yet i hear one insult
and all confidence shatters

- *focusing on the negative*

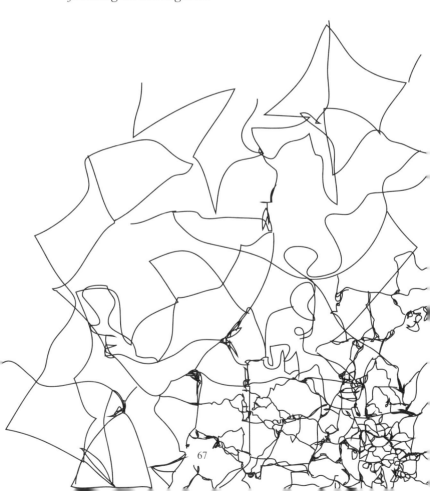

home

it began as a typical thursday from what i recall
sunlight kissed my eyelids good morning
i remember it exactly
climbing out of bed
making coffee to the sound of children playing outside
putting music on
loading the dishwasher
i remember placing flowers in a vase
in the middle of the kitchen table

only when my apartment was spotless
did i step into the bathtub
wash yesterday out of my hair
dress myself like
the walls of my home
were decorated with frames bookshelves photos
i hung a necklace around my neck
hooked earrings in
applied lipstick like paint
swept my hair back – just your typical thursday

we ended up at a get-together with friends
at the end you asked if i need a ride home and
i said *yes* cause our dads work at the same company
and you'd been to my place for dinner many times

but i should have known
when you began to confuse
kind conversation with flirtation
when you told me to let my hair down
when instead of driving me home toward
the bright intersection of lights and life – you took a left
to the road that led nowhere
i asked where we were going
you asked if i was afraid
my voice threw itself over the edge of my throat
landed at the bottom of my belly and hid for months
all the different parts in me turned the lights off
shut the blinds
locked the doors
while i hid at the back of
some upstairs closet of my mind as
someone broke the windows – you
kicked the front door in – you
someone took everything

it was you
who dived into me with a fork and a knife
eyes glinting with starvation
like you hadn't eaten in weeks
i was a hundred and ten pounds of fresh meat
you skinned and gutted with your fingers
like you were scraping the inside of a cantaloupe clean
as i screamed for my mother
you nailed my wrists to the ground
turned my breasts into bruised fruit

this home is empty now
no gas
no electricity
no running water
the food is rotten
from head to foot i am layered in dust
fruit flies. webs. bugs.
someone call the plumber
my stomach is backed up
i've been vomiting since
call the electrician
my eyes won't light up
call the cleaners
to wash me up and hang me to dry

when you broke into my home
it never felt like mine again
i can't even let a lover in without getting sick
i lose sleep after the first date
lose my appetite
become more bone and less skin
forget to breathe
every night my bedroom becomes
a psych ward where panic attacks
turn men into doctors to keep me calm
every lover who touches me – feels like you
their fingers – you
mouths – you
until they're not the ones on top of me anymore
– it's you

and i'm so tired of
doing things your way – it isn't working
i've spent years trying to figure out
how i could have stopped it
but the sun can't stop the storm from coming
the tree can't stop the axe
i can't blame myself for having a hole the size
of your manhood in my chest anymore
it's too heavy to carry your guilt – i'm setting it down
i'm tired of decorating this place with your shame
as if it belongs to me
it's too much to walk around with
what your hands have done
if it's not my hands that have done it

the truth comes to me suddenly – after years of rain
the truth comes like sunlight
pouring through an open window
it takes a long time to get here
but it all comes full circle
it takes a broken person to come
searching for meaning between my legs
it takes a complete. whole.
perfectly designed person to survive it
it takes monsters to steal souls
and fighters to reclaim them
this home is what i came into this world with
was the first home
will be the last home
you can't take it
there is no space for you

no welcome mat
no extra bedrooms
i'm opening all the windows
airing it out
putting flowers in a vase in the middle of the kitchen table
lighting a candle
loading the dishwasher with all my thoughts
until they're spotless
scrubbing the countertops
and then i plan to step into the bathtub
wash yesterday out of my hair
dress my body in gold
put music on
sit back
put my feet up
and enjoy this typical thursday

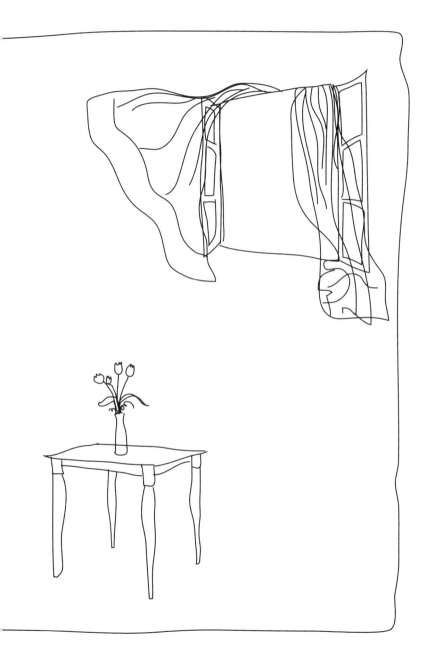

when snow falls
i long for grass
when grass grows
i walk all over it
when leaves change colour
i beg for flowers
when flowers bloom
i pick them

- *unappreciative*

tell them i was the
warmest place you knew
and how you turned me cold

at home that night
i filled the bathtub with scorching water
tossed in spearmint from the garden
two tablespoons almond oil
some milk and honey
a pinch of salt
rose petals from the neighbour's lawn
i soaked myself in the potion
desperate to wash the dirty off
the first hour
i picked pine needles from my hair
counted them one two three
lined them up on their backs
the second hour
i wept
a howling escaped me
who knew girl could become beast
in the third hour
i found bits of him on bits of me
the sweat was not mine
the white between my legs
not mine
the bite marks
not mine
the smell
not mine
the blood
mine
the fourth hour i prayed

it felt like you threw me
so far from myself
i've been trying to find my way back ever since

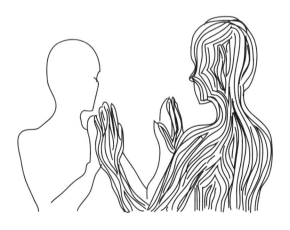

i reduced my body to aesthetics
forgot the work it did to keep me alive
with every beat and breath
declared it a grand failure for not looking like theirs
searched everywhere for a miracle
foolish enough to not realise
i was already living in one

the irony of loneliness
is we all feel it
at the same time

- *together*

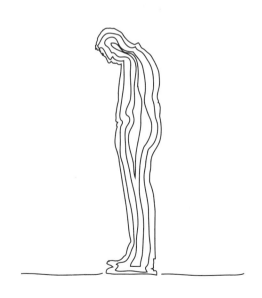

my girlhood was too much hair
thin limbs coated in velvet
it was neighbourhood tradition
for the other young girls and i
to frequent at-home salons
set up in shabby basements
run by women who were
my mother's age
had my mother's skin
but looked nothing like my simple mother
they had brown skin with
yellow hair meant for white skin
streaks like zebras
slits for eyebrows
i looked at my own caterpillars with shame
and dreamt mine would be that thin

as i sat timidly in the makeshift waiting area
i sang along with the bollywood music video
playing on a tiny television screen
while the other women were
getting their legs waxed or hair dyed

when auntie calls me in
i walk into the room
and make small talk
she leaves to let me undress
i slide my pants and underwear off
lie down on the spa table
she returns and positions my legs
like an open butterfly

soles of feet together
knees pointing in opposite directions

first the disinfectant wipe
then the cold jelly
how is school and *what are you studying* she asks
turns the laser on
places the head of the handle on my pubic bone
and just like that
the hair follicles around
my clitoris begin burning
i wince with each zap
trembling in pain

why do i do this
why do i punish my body
for being exactly as it's meant to be
halfway through the regret i think of him
and how i'm too embarrassed to be naked
unless it's clean

- *basement aesthetician*

we have been dying
since we got here
and forgot to enjoy the view

- *live fully*

you were mine
and my life was full
you are no longer mine
and my life
is full

my eyes
make mirrors out of
every reflective surface they pass
searching for something beautiful looking back
my ears fish for compliments and praise
but no matter how far they go looking
nothing is enough for me
i go to clinics and department stores
for pretty potions and new techniques
i've tried the lasers
i've tried the facials
i've tried the blades and expensive creams
for a hopeful minute they fill me
make me glow from cheek to cheek
but as soon as i feel beautiful
their magic disappears suddenly
where am i supposed to find it
i am willing to pay any price
for a beauty that makes heads turn
every moment day and night

- *a never-ending search*

this place makes me
the kind of exhausted that has
nothing to do with sleep
and everything to do with
the people around me

- introvert

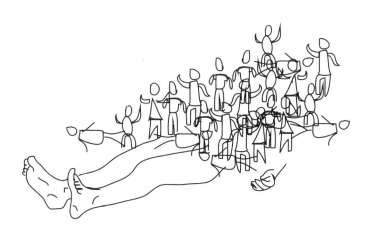

you must see no worth in yourself
if you find me worth less
after you've touched me
as if your hands on my body
magnify you and reduce me
to nothing

- *worth is not something we transfer*

you do not just wake up and become the butterfly

- *growth is a process*

i am having a difficult time right now
comparing myself to other people
i am stretching myself thin trying to be them
making fun of my face like my father
calling it ugly
starving out this premature double chin before it
melts into my shoulders like candle wax
fixing the bags under my eyes that carry the rape
bookmarking surgical procedures for my nose
there is so much that needs tending to
can you point me in the right direction
i need to take this body off
which way back to the womb

like the rainbow
after the rain
joy will reveal itself
after sorrow

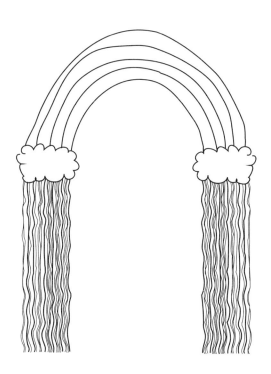

no was a bad word in my home
no was met with the lash
erased from our vocabulary
beaten out of our backs
till we became well-behaved kids
who obediently nodded *yes* to everything

when he climbed on top of me
every part of my body wanted to stop him
but i couldn't say *no* to save my life
when i screamed
all that escaped me was silence
i heard *no* pounding her fist
on the roof of my mouth
begging to let her out
but i hadn't put up the exit sign
never built the emergency staircase
there was no trapdoor for *no* to escape from

what use was obedience then
when there were hands
that were not mine
inside me

- *how can i verbalise consent as an adult if i was*
  never allowed to as a child

despite knowing
they won't be here for long
they still choose to live
their brightest lives

- *sunflowers*

when you find her
tell her not a day goes by
when i do not think of her
that girl who thinks you are
everything she asked for
when you bounce her off the walls
and she cries
tell her i cry with her too
the sound of drywall crunching into itself
as it's beaten with her head
also lives in my ears
tell her to run to me
i have already unscrewed
my front door off its frame
opened all the windows
inside there is a warm bath running
she does not need your kind of love
i am proof she will get out
and find her way back to herself
if i could survive you
so will she

parts of my body still ache
from the first time they were touched

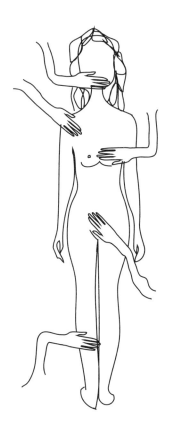

the art of growing

i felt beautiful until the age of twelve
when my body began to ripen like new fruit
and suddenly
the men looked at my newborn hips with salivating lips
the boys didn't want to play tag at recess
they wanted to touch all the new
and unfamiliar parts of me
the parts i didn't know how to wear
didn't know how to carry
tried to bury in my rib cage

boobs they said
and i hated that word
hated that i was embarrassed to say it
that even though it was referring to my body
it didn't belong to me
it belonged to them
and they repeated it like
they were meditating upon it
boobs he said
let me see yours
there is nothing worth seeing here but guilt and shame
i try to rot into the earth below my feet
but i'm still standing one foot across
from his hooked fingers
and when he charges to feast on my half-moons
i bite into his forearm and decide i hate this body
i must've done something terrible to deserve it

when i go home i tell my mother
the men outside are starving
she tells me
i must not dress with my breasts hanging
said *the boys will get hungry if they see fruit*
said i should sit with my legs closed
like a woman oughta
or the men will get angry and fight
said i can avoid all this trouble
if i just learn to act like a lady
but the problem is
that doesn't even make sense
i can't wrap my head around the fact
that i have to convince half the world's population
my body is not their bed
i am busy learning the consequences of womanhood
when i should be learning science and math instead
i like cartwheels and gymnastics so i can't imagine
walking around with my thighs pressed together
like they're hiding a secret
as if the acceptance of my own body parts
will invite thoughts of lust in their heads
i will not subject myself to their ideology
cause slut shaming is rape culture
virgin praising is rape culture
i am not a mannequin in the window
of your favourite shop
you can't dress me up or
throw me out when i am worn
you are not a cannibal

your actions are not my responsibility
you will control yourself

so the next time i go to school
and the boys hoot at my backside
i push them down
foot over their necks
and defiantly say
boobs
and the look in their eyes is priceless

when the world comes crashing at your feet
it's okay to let others
help pick up the pieces
if we're present to take part in your happiness
when your circumstances are great
we are more than capable
of sharing your pain

- *community*

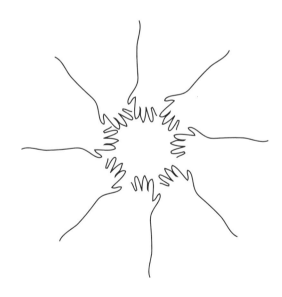

i do not weep
because i'm unhappy
i weep because i have everything
yet – i'm unhappy

let it go
let it leave
let it happen
nothing
in this world
was promised or
belonged to you anyway

- *all you own is yourself*

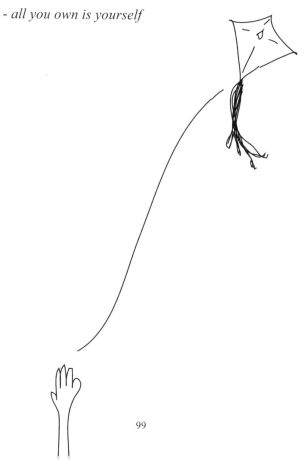

wish pure love and soft peace
upon the ones
who've been unkind to you
and move forward

- *this will free you both*

yes
it is possible
to hate and love someone
at the same time
i do it to myself
every day

somewhere along the way
i lost the self-love
and became my greatest enemy
i thought i'd seen the devil before
in the uncles who touched us as children
the mobs that burned our city to the ground
but i'd never seen someone as hungry
for my flesh as i was
i peeled my skin off just to feel awake
wore it inside out
sprinkled it with salt to punish myself
turmoil clotted my nerves
my blood curdled
i even tried to bury myself alive
but the dirt recoiled
you have already rotted it said
there is nothing left for me to do

- *self-hate*

the way you speak of yourself
the way you degrade yourself
into smallness
is abuse

- *self-harm*

when i hit the rock bottom
that exists after the rock bottom
and no rope or hand appeared
i wondered
what if nothing wants me
cause i do not want me
perhaps i am both the poison
and the antidote

first
i went for my words
the *i can't*s. the *i won't*s. the *i'm not good enough*s.
i lined them up and shot them dead
then i went for my thoughts
invisible and everywhere
there was no time to gather them one by one
i had to wash them out
i wove a linen cloth out of my hair
soaked it in a bowl of mint and lemon water
carried it in my mouth as i climbed
up my braid to the back of my head
down on my knees i began to wipe my mind clean
it took twenty-one days
my knees bruised but
i did not care
i was not given the breath
in my lungs to choke it out
i would scrub the self-hate off the bone
till it exposed love

- *self-love*

i have survived far too much to go quietly
let a meteor take me
call the thunder for backup
my death will be grand
the land will crack
the sun will eat itself
the day i leave

i want to honeymoon myself

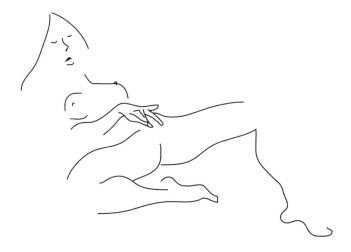

if i am the longest relationship of my life
shouldn't i nurture the same love
and forgiveness in myself
as i do in others

- *i am the person i lie in bed with each night*

what is stronger
than the human heart
which shatters over and over
and still lives

i woke up thinking the work was done
i would not have to practice today
how naive to think healing was that easy
when there is no end point
no finish line to cross

- *healing is everyday work*

you have so much
but are always hungry for more
stop looking up at everything you don't have
and look around at everything you do

- where the satisfaction lives

you can imitate a light like mine
but you cannot become it

and here you are living
despite it all

this is the recipe of life
said my mother
as she held me in her arms as i wept
think of those flowers you plant
in the garden each year
they will teach you
that people too
must wilt
fall
root
rise
in order to bloom

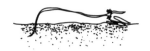

rupi kaur

rooting

they have no idea what it's like
to lose home at the risk of
never finding home again
to have your entire life
split between two lands and
become the bridge between two countries

- *immigrant*

look at what they've done
the earth cried to the moon
they've turned me into one entire bruise

- green and blue

you are an open wound
and we are standing
in a pool of your blood

- *refugee camp*

when it came to listening
my mother taught me silence
if you are drowning their voice with yours
how will you hear them she asked

when it came to speaking
she said *do it with commitment*
every word you say
is your own responsibility

when it came to being
she said *be tender and tough at once*
you need to be vulnerable to live fully
but rough enough to survive it all

when it came to choosing
she asked me to be thankful
for the choices i had that
she never had the privilege of making

- *lessons from mumma*

leaving her country
was not easy for my mother
i still catch her searching for it
in foreign films
and the international food aisle

as she sat in a costume of red and gold on her wedding
day. i wonder where she hid him. her brother. who had
died only a year before. she tells me how her wedding
was the saddest day of her life. how she hadn't finished
mourning yet. a year was not enough. there was no
way to grieve that quick. it felt like a blink. a breath.
before the news of his loss had sunk in. the wedding
decorations were up. the guests were strolling in. the
small talk. the rush. all mirrored his funeral too much.
it felt as though his body had just been carried away for
the cremation. when my father and his family arrived
for the wedding celebrations.

- *amrik singh (1959–1990)*

i am sorry this world
could not keep you safe
may your journey home
be a soft and peaceful one

- *rest in peace*

your legs buckle like a tired horse running for safety
drag them by the hips and move faster
you do not have the privilege to rest
in a country that wants to spit you out
you have to keep
going and going
and going
till you reach the water
hand over everything in your name
for a ticket onto the boat
next to a hundred others like you
packed like sardines
you tell the woman beside you
this boat is not strong enough to carry
this much sorrow to a shore
what does it matter she says
if drowning is easier than staying
how many people has this water drunk up
is it all one long cemetery
bodies buried without a country
perhaps the sea is your country
perhaps the boat sinks
because it is the only place that will take you

- *boat*

what if we get to their doors
and they slam them shut i ask

what are doors she says
when we've escaped the belly of death

borders
are man-made
they only divide us physically
don't let them make us
turn on each other

- *we are not enemies*

after the surgery
she tells me
how bizarre it is
that they just took out
the first home of her children

- hysterectomy february 2016

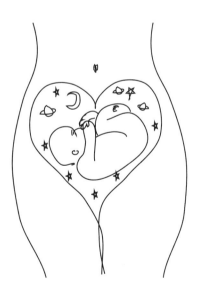

bombs brought entire cities
down to their knees today
refugees boarded boats knowing
their feet may never touch land again
police shot people dead for the colour of their skin
last month i visited an orphanage of
abandoned babies left on the curbside like waste
later at the hospital i watched a mother
lose both her child and her mind
somewhere a lover died
how can i refuse to believe
my life is anything short of a miracle
if amid all this chaos
i was given this life

- *circumstances*

perhaps we are all immigrants
trading one home for another
first we leave the womb for air
then the suburbs for the filthy city
in search of a better life
some of us just happen to leave entire countries

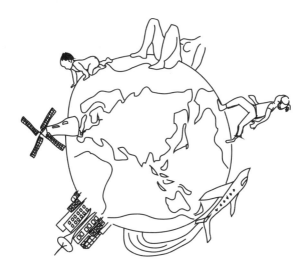

my god
is not waiting inside a church
or sitting above the temple's steps
my god
is the refugee's breath as she's running
living in the starving child's belly
is the heartbeat of the protest
my god
does not rest between pages
written by holy men
my god
rests in the sweaty thighs
of women's bodies sold for money
was last seen washing the homeless man's feet
my god
isn't as unreachable as
they'd like you to think
my god
is beating inside us infinitely

advice i would've given
my mother on her wedding day

1. you are allowed to say *no*

2. years ago his father beat the language of love
    out of your husband's back
    he will never know how to say it
    but his actions prove he loves you

3. go with him
    when he enters your body and goes to that place
    sex is not dirty

4. no matter how many times his family brings it up
    do not have the abortion just because i'm a girl
    lock the relatives out and swallow the key
    he will not hate you

5. take your journals and paintings
    across the ocean when you leave
    these will remind you who you are
    when you get lost amid new cities
    they will also remind your children
    you had an entire life before them

6. when your husbands are off
    working at the factories
    make friends with all the other
    lonely women in the apartment complex
    this loneliness will cut a person in half
    you will need each other to stay alive

7. your husband and children will take from your plate
   we will emotionally and mentally starve you
   all of it is wrong
   don't let us convince you that
   sacrificing yourself is
   how you must show love

8. when your mother dies
   fly back for the funeral
   money comes and goes
   a mother is once in a lifetime

9. you are allowed to spend
   a couple dollars on a coffee
   i know there was a time when
   we could not afford it
   but we are okay now. breathe.

10. you can't speak english fluently
    or operate a computer or cell phone
    we did that to you. it is not your fault.
    you are not any less than the
    other mothers with their
    flashy phones and designer clothing
    we confined you to the four walls of this home
    and worked you to the bone
    you have not been your own property for decades

11. there was no rule book for how
    to be the first woman in your lineage
    to raise a family on a strange land by yourself

12. you are the person i look up to most

13. when i am about to shatter
    i think of your strength
    and harden

14. i think you are a magician

15. i want to fill the rest of your life with ease

16. you are the hero of heroes
    the god of gods

in a dream
i saw my mother
with the love of her life
and no children
it was the happiest i'd ever seen her

- *what if*

you split the world
into pieces and
called them countries
declared ownership on
what never belonged to you
and left the rest with nothing

- *colonise*

my parents never sat us down in the evenings to share
stories of their younger days. one was always working.
the other too tired. perhaps being an immigrant does
that to you.

the cold terrain of the north engulfed them. their bodies
hard at work paying in blood and sweat for their
citizenship. perhaps the weight of the new world was
too much. and the pain and sorrow of the old was better
left buried.

i do wish i had unburied it though. i wish i'd pried their
silence apart like a closed envelope. i wish i'd found a
small opening at its very edge. pushed a finger inside
and gently tore it open. they had an entire life before
me which i'm a stranger to. and it would be my greatest
regret to see them leave this place before i even got to
know them.

my voice
is the offspring
of two countries colliding
what is there to be ashamed of
if english
and my mother tongue
made love
my voice
is her father's words
and mother's accent
what does it matter if
my mouth carries two worlds

- *accent*

for years they were separated by oceans
left with nothing but photographs of each other
smaller than passport-size photos
hers was tucked into a golden locket
his slipped inside his wallet
at the end of the day
studying these was their only intimacy

this was a time long before computers
when families in that part of the world
had not seen a telephone or laid their
almond eyes on a coloured television screen

long before you and me

as the wheels of the plane touched tarmac
she wondered if this was the right place
had she boarded the correct flight
should've asked the air hostess twice
like her husband suggested

walking into baggage claim
her heart beat so heavy
she thought it might fall out
eyes darting in every direction
searching for what to do next
when suddenly
right there
in the flesh
he stood
not a mirage – a man
first came relief

then bewilderment
they'd waited tirelessly for this reunion
but now she'd forgotten the words
she had rehearsed for years
shadows circled his eyes

his shoulders carried an invisible weight
it looked like the life
had been drained out of him
where was the person she had wed
she wondered while reaching for the golden locket
with the photo of the man
her husband did not look like anymore

- *the new world had drained him*

what if
there isn't enough time
to give her what she deserves
do you think
if i begged the sky hard enough
my mother's soul would
return to me as my daughter
so i can give her
the comfort she gave me
my whole life

i want to go back in time and sit beside her. document
her in a home movie so my eyes can spend the rest of
their lives witnessing a miracle. the one whose life i
never think of before mine. i want to know what she
laughed about with friends. in the village within houses
of mud and brick. surrounded by acres of mustard plant
and sugarcane. i want to sit with the teenage version
of my mother. ask about her dreams. become her
pleated braid. the black kohl caressing her eyelids. the
flour neatly packed into her fingertips. a page of her
schoolbooks. even to be a single thread of her cotton
dress would be the greatest gift.

- *to witness a miracle*

1790

he takes the newborn girl from his wife
and walks out of their bedroom
cradles the baby's head with his left hand
and gently snaps her neck with his right

1890

a wet towel to wrap her in
grains of rice and
sand in the nose
a mother shares the trick with her daughter-in-law
i had to do it she says
as did my mother
and her mother before her

1990

a newspaper article reads
a hundred baby girls were found buried
behind a doctor's house in a neighbouring village
she wonders if that's where he took her
she imagines her daughter becoming the soil
fertilising the roots that feed this country

1998

oceans away in a toronto basement
a doctor performs an illegal abortion
on an indian woman who already has a daughter
one is burden enough she says

2006
it's easier than you think my aunties tell my mother
they know a family
who've done it three times
they know a clinic. they could get mumma the number.
the doctor even prescribes pills that guarantee a boy.
they worked for the woman down the street they say
now she has three sons

2012
twelve hospitals in the toronto area
refuse to reveal a baby's gender to expecting families
until the thirtieth week of pregnancy
all twelve hospitals are located in areas with high
south asian immigrant populations

- female infanticide | female feticide

remember the body
of your community
breathe in the people
who sewed you whole
it is you who became yourself
but those before you
are a part of your fabric

- *honour the roots*

when they buried me alive
i dug my way
out of the ground
with palm and fist
i howled so loud
the earth rose in fear and
the dirt began to levitate
my whole life has been an uprising
one burial after another

- i will find my way out of you just fine

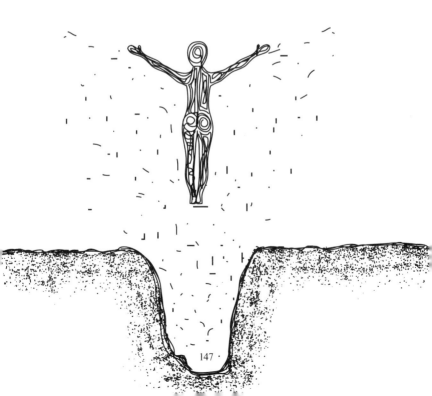

my mother sacrificed her dreams
so i could dream

broken english

i think about the way my father
pulled the family out of poverty
without knowing what a vowel was
and my mother raised four children
without being able to construct
a perfect sentence in english
a discombobulated couple
who landed in the new world with hopes
that left the bitter taste of rejection in their mouths
no family
no friends
just man and wife
two university degrees that meant nothing
one mother tongue that was broken now
one swollen belly with a baby inside
a father worrying about jobs and rent
cause no matter what this baby was coming
and they thought to themselves for a split second
was it worth it to put all of our money
into the dream of a country
that is swallowing us whole

papa looks at his woman's eyes
and sees loneliness living where the iris was
wants to give her a home in a country that looks at her
with the word *visitor* wrapped around its tongue
on their wedding day

she left an entire village to be his wife
now she left an entire country to be a warrior
and when the winter came
they had nothing but the heat of their own bodies
to keep the coldness out

like two brackets they faced one another
to hold the dearest parts of them – their children – close
they turned a suitcase full of clothes into a life
and regular paychecks
to make sure the children of immigrants
wouldn't hate them for being the children of immigrants
they worked too hard
you can tell by their hands
their eyes are begging for sleep
but our mouths were begging to be fed
and that is the most artistic thing i have ever seen
it is poetry to these ears
that have never heard what passion sounds like
and my mouth is full of *like*s and *um*s when
i look at their masterpiece
cause there are no words in the english language
that can articulate that kind of beauty
i can't compact their existence into twenty-six letters
and call it a description
i tried once
but the adjectives needed to describe them
don't even exist
so instead i ended up with pages and pages
full of words followed by commas and

more words and more commas
only to realise there are some things
in the world so infinite
they could never use a full stop

so how dare you mock your mother
when she opens her mouth and
broken english spills out
don't be ashamed of the fact that
she split through countries to be here
so you wouldn't have to cross a shoreline
her accent is thick like honey
hold it with your life
it's the only thing she has left of home
don't you stomp on that richness
instead hang it up on the walls of museums
next to dali and van gogh
her life is brilliant and tragic
kiss the side of her tender cheek
she already knows what it feels like
to have an entire nation laugh when she speaks
she is more than our punctuation and language
we might be able to paint pictures and write stories
but she made an entire world for herself

how is that for art

rising

on the first day of love
you wrapped me in the word *special*

you must remember it too
how the rest of the city slept
while we sat awakened for the first time
we hadn't touched yet
but we managed to travel in and out
of each other with our words
our limbs dizzying with enough electricity
to form half a sun
we drank nothing that night
but i was intoxicated
i went home and thought
are we soul mates

i feel apprehensive
cause falling into you
means falling out of him and
i had not prepared for that

- *forward*

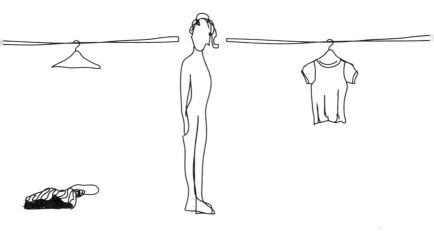

how do i welcome in kindness
when i have only practiced
spreading my legs for the terrifying
what am i to do with you
if my idea of love is violence
but you are sweet
if your concept of passion is eye contact
but mine is rage
how can i call this intimacy
if i crave sharp edges
but your edges aren't even edges
they are soft landings
how do i teach myself
to accept a healthy love
if all i've ever known is pain

i will welcome
a partner
who is my equal

never feel guilty for starting again

the middle place is strange
the part between them and the next
is an awakening from how you saw to
how you will see
this is where their charm wears off
where they are no longer
the god you made them out to be
when the pedestal you carved out of your
bone and teeth no longer serves them
they are unmasked and made mortal again

- the middle place

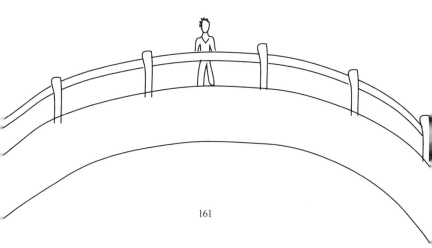

when you start loving someone new
you laugh at the indecisiveness of love
remember when you were sure
the last one was *the one*
and now here you are
redefining *the one* all over again

- *a fresh love is a gift*

i do not need the kind of love
that is draining
i want someone
who energises me

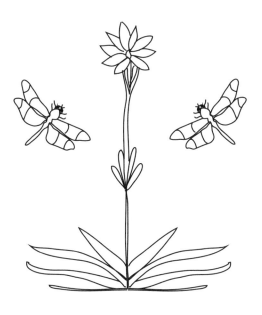

i am trying to not
make you pay for their mistakes
i am trying to teach myself
you are not responsible
for the wound
how can i punish you
for what you have not done
you wear my emotions
like a decorated army vest
you are not cold or
savage or hungry
you are medicinal

- *you are not them*

he makes sure to look right at me
as he places his electric fingers on my skin
how does that feel he asks
commanding my attention
responding is out of the question
i quiver with anticipation
excited and terrified for what's to come
he smiles
knows this is what satisfaction looks like
i am a switchboard
he is the circuits
my hips move with his – rhythmic
my voice isn't my own when i moan – it is music
like fingers on a violin string
he sparks enough electricity within me to power a city
when we finish i look right at him
and tell him
that was magic

when i walked into the coffee shop and saw you. my
body didn't react like it had the first time we ran into
each other. i expected my legs to freeze up. for my
heart to abandon me. to fall to the ground crying at
your sight. but not this time. there was no movement
inside when we locked eyes. you were just a regular
guy with your regular clothes and regular coffee.
nothing profound about you.

my body must've cleansed itself of you long ago. must
have gotten tired of me acting like i'd lost the best thing
that could've happened. must've wrung the insecurities
out while i wallowed in pity.

that day i had no makeup on. my hair was all over
the place. dressed in my brother's old t-shirt and
sweatpants. yet i felt like a gleaming siren. a mermaid.
i did a little dance in the car on the drive home. cause
even though we were both under the same roof of that
coffee shop. i was still solar systems away from you.

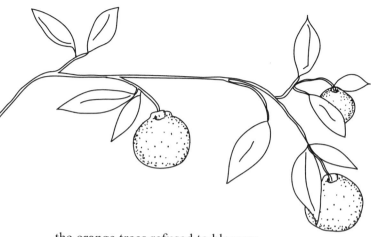

the orange trees refused to blossom
unless we bloomed first
when we met
they wept tangerines
can't you tell
the earth has waited
its whole life for us
even the sun
shone for seven days straight

- *celebration*

why am i always running in circles
between wanting you to want me
and when you want me
deciding it is too emotionally naked
for me to live with
why do i make loving me so difficult
as if you should never have to witness
the ghosts i have tucked under my breast
i used to be more open
when it came to matters like this my love

- *if only we'd met when i was that willing*

i could not contain myself any longer
i ran to the ocean
in the middle of the night
and confessed my love for you to the water
as i finished telling her
the salt in her body became sugar

(ode to sobha singh's *sohni mahiwal*)

i say *maybe this is a mistake. maybe we need more than love to make this work.*

you place your lips on mine. when our faces are buzzing with the ecstasy of kissing you say *tell me that isn't right.* and as much as i'd like to think with my head. my racing heart is all that makes sense. there. right there is the answer you're looking for. in my loss of breath. my lack of words. my silence. my inability to speak means you've filled my stomach with so many butterflies that even if this is a mistake. it could only be right to be this wrong with you.

a
man
who cries

- *a gift*

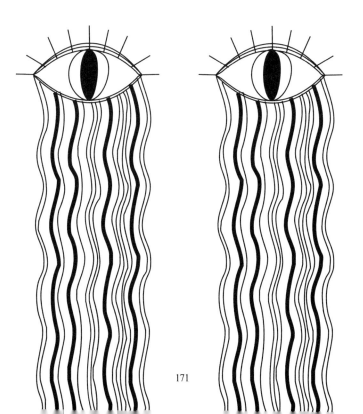

if i'm going to share my life with a partner
it would be foolish not to ask myself
twenty years from now
is this person going to be
someone i still laugh with
or am i just distracted by their charm
do i see us evolving into
new people by the decade
or does the growing ever come to a pause
i don't want to be distracted
by the looks or the money
i want to know if they pull
the best or the worst out of me
deep at the core are our values the same
in thirty years will we still
jump into bed like we're twenty
can i picture us in old age
conquering the world
like we've got young blood running in our veins

- *checklist*

what is it with you and sunflowers he asks

i point to the field of yellow outside
sunflowers worship the sun i tell him
only when it arrives do they rise
when the sun leaves
they bow their heads in mourning
that is what the sun does to those flowers
it's what you do to me

- the sun and her flowers

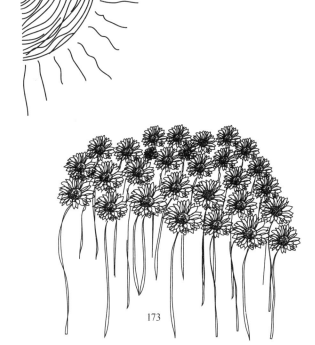

sometimes
i stop myself from
saying the words out loud
as if leaving my mouth too often
might wear them down

- *i love you*

the most important conversations
we'll have are with our fingers
when yours nervously graze mine
for the first time during dinner

they'll tighten with fear
when you ask to see me again next week
but as soon as i say yes
they'll stretch out in ease

when they grasp one another
while we're beneath the sheets
the two of us will pretend
we're not weak in the knees

when i get angry
they'll pulse with bitter cries
but when they tremble for forgiveness
you'll see what apologies look like

and when one of us is dying
on a hospital bed at eighty-five
your fingers will grip mine
to say things words can't describe

- *fingers*

this morning
i told the flowers
what i'd do for you
and they blossomed

there is no place
i end and you begin
when your body
is in my body
we are one person

- *sex*

if i had to walk to get to you
it would take eight hundred and twenty-six hours
on bad days i think about it
what i might do if the apocalypse comes
and the planes stop flying
there is so much time to think
so much empty space wanting to be consumed
but no intimacy around to consume it
it feels like being stuck at a train station
and waiting and waiting and waiting
for the one with your name on it
when the moon rises on this coast
but the sun still burns shamelessly on yours
i crumble knowing even our skies are different
we have been together so long
but have we really been together if
your touch has not held me long enough
to imprint itself on my skin
i try my hardest to stay present
but without you here
everything at its best
is only mediocre

- long distance

i am
made of water
of course i am emotional

they should feel like home
a place that grounds your life
where you go to take the day off

- *the one*

the moon is responsible
for pulling tides
out of still water
darling
i am the still water
and you are the moon

the right one does not
stand in your way
they make space for you
to step forward

when you are
full
and i am
full
we are two suns

your voice does to me
what autumn does to trees
you call to say hello
and my clothes fall naturally

together we are an endless conversation

when death
takes my hand
i will hold you with the other
and promise to find you
in every lifetime

- *commitment*

it was as though
someone had slid ice cubes
down the back of my shirt

- *orgasm*

you have
been
inside me
before

- *another lifetime*

god must have kneaded you and i
from the same dough
rolled us out as one on the baking sheet
must have suddenly realised
how unfair it was
to put that much magic in one person
and sadly split that dough in two
how else is it that
when i look in the mirror
i am looking at you
when you breathe
my own lungs fill with air
that we just met but we
have known each other our whole lives
if we were not made as one to begin with

- *our souls are mirrors*

to be
two legs
on one body

- *a relationship*

you must have a
honeycomb
for a heart
how else
could a man
be this sweet

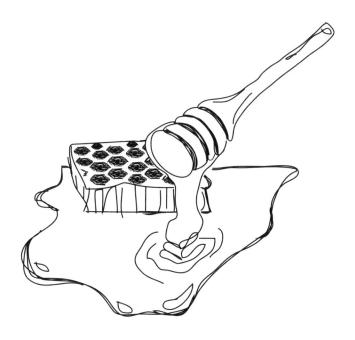

if you got any more beautiful
the sun would leave its place
and come for you

- *the chase*

it has been one of the greatest and most difficult years
of my life. i learned everything is temporary. moments.
feelings. people. flowers. i learned love is about giving.
everything. and letting it hurt. i learned vulnerability
is always the right choice because it is easy to be cold
in a world that makes it so very difficult to remain soft.
i learned all things come in twos. life and death. pain
and joy. salt and sugar. me and you. it is the balance of
the universe. it has been the year of hurting so bad but
living so good. making friends out of strangers. making
strangers out of friends. learning mint chocolate chip
ice cream will fix just about everything. and for the
pains it can't there will always be my mother's arms.
we must learn to focus on warm energy. always soak
our limbs in it and become better lovers to the world.
for if we can't learn to be kind to each other how will
we ever learn to be kind to the most desperate
parts of ourselves.

blooming

the universe took its time on you
crafted you to offer the world
something different from everyone else
when you doubt
how you were created
you doubt an energy greater than us both

- irreplaceable

when the first woman spread her legs
to let the first man in
what did he see
when she led him down the hallway
toward the sacred room
what sat waiting
what shook him so deeply
all confidence shattered

from then on
the first man
watched the first woman
every night and day
built a cage to keep her in
so she could sin no more
set fire to her books
called her *witch*
and shouted *whore*
until the evening came
when his tired eyes betrayed him

the first woman noticed it
as he unwillingly fell asleep
the quiet humming
the drumming
a knocking between her legs
a doorbell
a voice
a pulse

asking her to open up
and off her hand went running
down the hall
toward the sacred room
she found
god
the magician's wand
the snake's tongue
sitting inside her smiling

- *when the first woman drew magic with her fingers*

i will no longer
compare my path to others

- *i refuse to do a disservice to my life*

i am the product of all the ancestors getting together
and deciding these stories need to be told

many tried
but failed to catch me
i am the ghost of ghosts
everywhere and nowhere
i am magic tricks
within magic within magic
none have figured out
i am a world wrapped in worlds
folded in suns and moons
you can try but
you won't get your hands on me

upon my birth
my mother said
there is god in you
do you feel her dancing

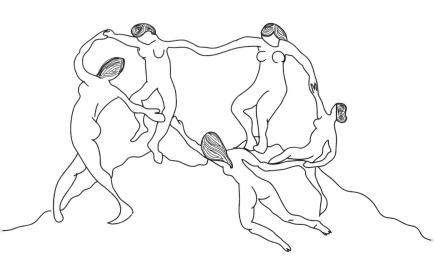

(ode to matisse's *dance*)

as a father of three daughters
it would have been normal
for him to push marriage on us
this has been the narrative for
the women in my culture for hundreds of years
instead he pushed education
knowing it would set us free
in a world that wanted to contain us
he made sure that we learned
to walk independently

there are far too many mouths here
but not enough of them are worth
what you're offering
give yourself to a few
and to those few
give heavily

- *invest in the right people*

i am of the earth
and to the earth i shall return once more
life and death are old friends
and i am the conversation between them
i am their late-night chatter
their laughter and tears
what is there to be afraid of
if i am the gift they give to each other
this place never belonged to me anyway
i have always been theirs

to hate
is an easy lazy thing
but to love
takes strength
everyone has
but not all are
willing to practice

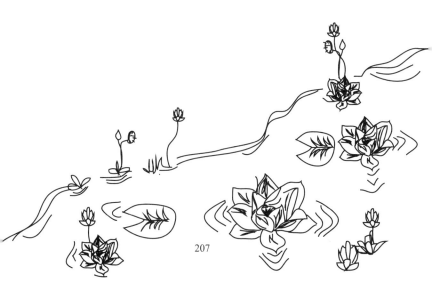

beautiful brown girl
your thick hair is a mink coat not all can afford
beautiful brown girl
your skin can't help but carry as much sun as possible
i know you hate the hyperpigmentation
but you are a magnet for the light
unibrow – the bridging of two worlds
vagina – so much darker than the rest of you
it is trying to hide a gold mine
you will have dark circles too early
appreciate the haloes
beautiful brown girl
you pull god out of their bellies

look down at your body
whisper
there is no home like you

- thank you

learning to not envy
someone else's blessings
is what grace looks like

i am the first woman in my lineage with freedom of
choice. to craft her future whichever way i choose. say
what is on my mind when i want to. without the whip of
the lash. there are hundreds of firsts i am thankful for.
that my mother and her mother and her mother before
her did not have the privilege of feeling. what an honour.
to be the first woman in the family who gets to taste her
desires. no wonder i'm starving to fill up on this life.
i have generations of bellies to eat for. the grandmothers
must be howling with laughter. huddled around a mud
stove in the afterlife. sipping on steaming glasses of
milky masala chai. how wild it must be for them to see
one of their own living so boldly.

(ode to amrita sher-gil's *village scene 1938*)

trust your body
it reacts to right and wrong
better than your mind does

- *it is speaking to you*

i stand
on the sacrifices
of a million women before me
thinking
what can i do
to make this mountain taller
so the women after me
can see farther

- *legacy*

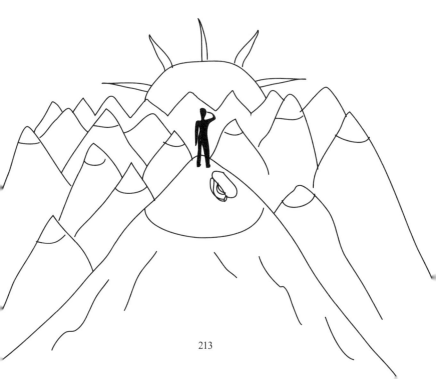

when i go from this place
dress the porch with garlands
as you would for a wedding my dear
pull the people from their homes
and dance in the streets
when death arrives
like a bride at the aisle
send me off in my brightest clothing
serve ice cream with rose petals to our guests
there's no reason to cry my dear
i have waited my whole life
for such a beauty to take
my breath away
when i go
let it be a celebration
for i have been here
i have lived
i have won at this game called life

- *funeral*

it was when i stopped searching for home within others
and lifted the foundations of home within myself
i found there were no roots more intimate
than those between a mind and body
that have decided to be whole

what good am i
if i do not fill the plates
of the ones who fed me
but fill the plates of strangers

- *family first*

even if they've been separated
they'll end up together
you can't keep lovers apart
no matter how much
i pluck and pull them
my eyebrows always
find their way
back to each other

- *unibrow*

a child and an elder
sat across from each other at a table
a cup of milk and tea before them

the elder asked the child if she was enjoying her life
the child answered yes life was good but
she couldn't wait to grow up
and do grown-up things

then the child asked the elder the same question
he too said life was good
but he'd give anything to go back to an age
when moving and dreaming were still possibilities

they both took a sip from their cups
but the child's milk had curdled
the elder's tea had grown bitter
there were tears running from their eyes

the day you have everything
i hope you remember
when you had nothing

she is not a porn category
or the type you look for
on a friday night
she is not needy or easy or weak

- *daddy issues is not a punch line*

i long to be a lily pad

i made change after change
on the road to perfection
but when i finally felt beautiful enough
their definition of beauty
suddenly changed

what if there was no finish line
and in my attempt to keep up
i lost the gifts i was born with
for a beauty so insecure
it couldn't commit to itself

- *the lies they sell*

rupi kaur

you want to keep
the blood and the milk hidden
as if the womb and breast
never fed you

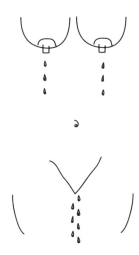

223

it is a trillion-dollar industry that would collapse
if we believed we were beautiful enough already

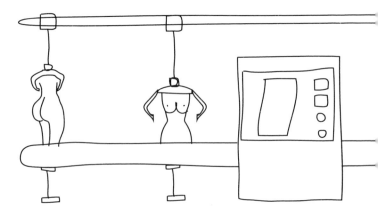

their concept of beauty
is manufactured
i am not

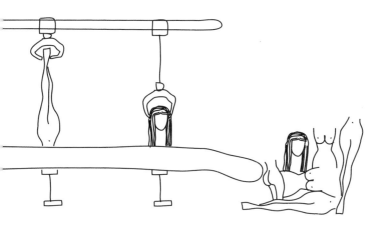

how do i shake this envy
when i see you doing well
sister how do i love myself enough to know
your accomplishments are not my failures

- *we are not each other's competition*

it is a blessing
to be the colour of earth
do you know how often
flowers confuse me for home

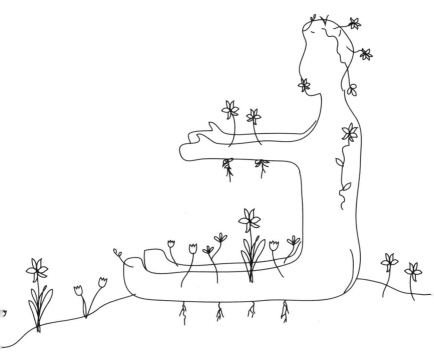

we need more love
not from men
but from ourselves
and each other

- *medicine*

you are a mirror
if you continue to starve yourself of love
you'll only meet people who'll starve you too
if you soak yourself in love
the universe will hand you those
who'll love you too

- *a simple math*

.

how much
or how little
clothing she has on
has nothing to do with how free she is

- *covered | uncovered*

there are mountains growing
beneath our feet
that cannot be contained
all we've endured
has prepared us for this
bring your hammers and fists
we have a glass ceiling to shatter

- let's leave this place roofless

231

it isn't blood that makes you my sister
it's how you understand my heart
as though you carry it
in your body

what is the greatest lesson a woman should learn

that since day one
she's already had everything she needs within herself
it's the world that convinced her she did not

they convinced me
i only had a few good years left
before i was replaced by a girl younger than me
as though men yield power with age
but women grow into irrelevance
they can keep their lies
for i have just gotten started
i feel as though i just left the womb
my twenties are the warm-up
for what i'm really about to do
wait till you see me in my thirties
now that will be a proper introduction
to the nasty. wild. woman in me.
how can i leave before the party's started
rehearsals begin at forty
i ripen with age
i do not come with an expiry date
and now
for the main event
curtains up at fifty
let's begin the show

- *timeless*

to heal
you have to
get to the root
of the wound
and kiss it all the way up

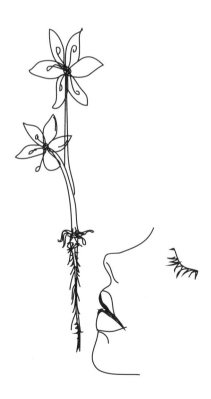

they threw us in a pit to end each other
so they wouldn't have to
starved us of space so long
we had to eat each other up to stay alive
look up
look up
look up
to catch them looking down at us
we have to stop fighting each other
cause the real monster is too big
to take down alone

when my daughter is living in my belly
i will speak to her like
she's already changed the world
she will walk out of me on a red carpet
fully equipped with the knowledge
that she's capable of
anything she sets her mind to

(ode to raymond douillet's *a short tour and farewell*)

now
is not the time
to be quiet
or make room for you
when we have had no room at all
now
is our time
to be mouthy
get as loud as we need
to be heard

representation
is vital
otherwise the butterfly
surrounded by a group of moths
unable to see itself
will keep trying to become the moth

- *representation*

take the compliment
do not shy away from
another thing that belongs to you

our work should equip
the next generation of women
to outdo us in every field
this is the legacy we'll leave behind

- *progress*

the road to changing the world
is never-ending

- *pace yourself*

i love you too much
to remain quiet as you weep
watch me rise to kiss the poison out of you
i resist the temptation
of my tired feet
and keep marching
with tomorrow in one hand
and a fist in the other
i will carry you to freedom

- *love letter to the world*

have your eyes ever fallen upon a beast like me
i have the spine of a mulberry tree
the neck of a sunflower
sometimes i am the desert
at times the rain forest
but always the wild
my belly brims over the waistband of my pants
each strand of hair frizzing out like a lifeline
it took a long time to become
such a sweet rebellion
back then i refused to water my roots
till i realised
if i am the only one
who can be the wilderness
then let me be the wilderness
the tree trunk cannot become the branch
the jungle cannot become the garden
so why should i

- *it is so full here in myself*

many try
but cannot tell the difference
between a marigold and my skin
both of them an orange sun
blinding the ones who have not learned to love the light

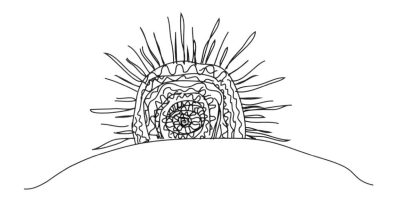

if you have never
stood with the oppressed
there is still time

- *lift them*

the year is done. i spread the past three hundred
sixty-five days before me on the living room carpet.

here is the month i decided to shed everything not
deeply committed to my dreams. the day i refused to be
a victim to the self-pity. here is the week i slept in the
garden. the spring i wrung the self-doubt by its neck.
hung your kindness up. took down the calendar.
the week i danced so hard my heart learned to float above
water again. the summer i unscrewed all the mirrors
from their walls. no longer needed to see myself to feel
seen. combed the weight out of my hair.

i fold the good days up and place them in my back
pocket for safekeeping. draw the match. cremate the
unnecessary. the light of the fire warms my toes.
i pour myself a glass of warm water to cleanse myself
for january. here i go. stronger and wiser into the new.

there is
nothing left
to worry about
the sun and her flowers are here.

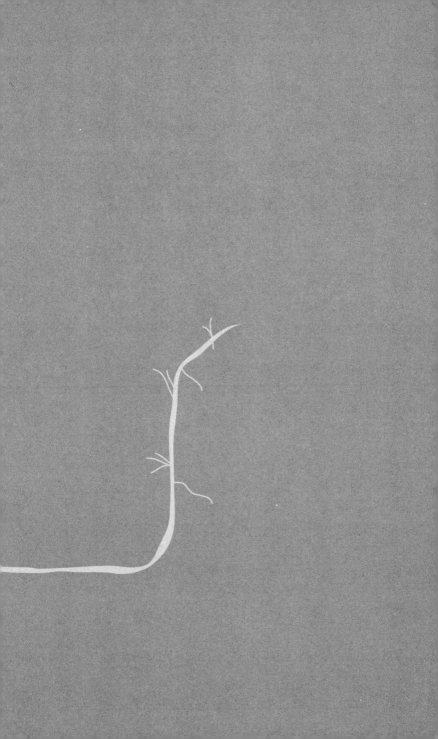

and then there are days when the simple act of
breathing leaves you exhausted. it seems easier to
give up on this life. the thought of disappearing
brings you peace. for so long i was lost in a
place where there was no sun. where there grew
no flowers. but every once in a while out of the
darkness something i loved would emerge and
bring me to life again. witnessing a starry sky.
the lightness of laughing with old friends.
a reader who told me the poems had saved their
life. yet here i was struggling to save my own.
my darlings. living is difficult. it is difficult for
everybody. but we must resist the urge of
succumbing to those difficulties. refuse to bow
before bad days. bad months or bad years. our eyes
are starving to feast on this world. there are too
many turquoise bodies of water left for us to dive
into. there is family. blood or chosen. the possibility
of falling in love. with people and places. hills
high as the moon. valleys rolling into new worlds.
road trips. i find it deeply important to accept that
we are not the masters of this place. we are her
visitors. so like the guests that we are. let's enjoy
this place like a garden. let us treat it with a gentle
hand. so the ones after us can enjoy it too. and
when the darkness comes. let's find our own sun.
grow our own flowers. the universe delivered us
with the light and the seeds. we might not hear it
at times but the music is always on. it just needs
to be turned a little louder. for as long as there is
breath in our lungs — we must keep dancing.

rupi kaur is a poet. artist. and performer. as a 21-year-old university student rupi wrote. illustrated. and self-published her first poetry collection *milk and honey*. next came its artistic sibling *the sun and her flowers*. these collections have sold over 8 million copies and have been translated into over 40 languages. *home body* is her third collection of poetry. rupi's work touches on love. loss. trauma. healing. femininity. and migration. she feels most at home when creating art or performing her poetry onstage. learn more at www.rupikaur.com.

the sun and her flowers is a
collection of poetry about
grief
self-abandonment
honouring one's roots
love
and empowering oneself
it is split into five chapters
wilting. falling. rooting. rising. and blooming.

- *about the book*